The PRIVATE thoughts and prayers of:

Date:

Dear God, Let's Talk About YOU

written by
Karen Ann Moore

illustrated by
Amy Wummer

Standard
PUBLISHING
CINCINNATI, OHIO

Scriptures quoted from *The Holy Bible, New Century Version*®, Copyright © 1987, 1988,
1991 by Word Publishing, a division of Thomas Nelson, Inc. Used by permission.

Published in association with the literary agency of Alive Communications, Inc.,
7680 Goddard Street, Suite 200, Colorado Springs, Colorado, 80920.

ISBN 0-7847-1247-6

09 08 07 06 05 04 03   9 8 7 6 5 4 3 2 1

When you pray to God, he will listen.

Philippians 4:6 says,
"Do not worry about anything, but pray and ask God for everything you need."

Prayer is a special gift from God. It's your way to connect with God and share with him about your life, your feelings, and even your questions.

Do you ever have questions for God? Have you ever heard something or read something in the Bible that seemed confusing or difficult? This book can help you!

Each part of this book looks at an issue or a difficult question that kids—maybe even you—might have. All you have to do is turn to the question that you're wondering about. You'll find out what the Bible says about that issue and find some ideas for how to pray about it.

Then ask God your question in prayer. By writing out prayers in the journal sections of this book, you can hand your concerns over to God. Everything that you share with God in prayer—even your questions—brings you closer to him.

Who Is God?

The Bible tells us God is Creator, Father, Jehovah, and the Almighty. But even those names don't tell us everything about God. Prayers in this section will help you discover God for yourself, perhaps in a different way than before. God wants you to know him, so ask him to show himself to you.

Talking to God

When you were little, you may have learned to talk to God with simple prayers at bedtime or at dinner. Now you're older and ready to share even more of your heart with God. This part is devoted to helping you get better at talking to God.

God's Word

The Bible is the amazing story of God's love for his creation. It has great adventure stories, love stories, and heroic tales. But it's more than just stories. The Bible is your key to understanding who God is and what God wants for your life. God's Word is like a road map because it helps you as you journey through life.

God and Me

God created this big, big universe . . . but then he went on to create you and me. He made beautiful stars and vast oceans, but he wasn't satisfied until he added people he could love. People are God's greatest work.

God and My Feelings

Sometimes you feel glad to see your friends. Sometimes you feel angry or disappointed with them. What feelings do you have for God? God created you—feelings and all. Whatever you feel, share it with God.

My teacher asked our class to name a person who is powerful. We named the president and Superman. Another person said God. Wow! That started us talking about what *power* really is. Sometimes it seems like there are lots of powerful people in the world who have control over other people. Does God still show his power today like he did when he started the world?

signed,

Just Wondering

MESSAGE TO GOD

Dear God, I believe that you are all-powerful. I just wonder if you're still doing things today like you did when you created everything. Amen.

pOwEr aNd SupEr-PoWer

❀ Superman: faster than a speeding bullet; God: creator of time itself

❀ Batman: comes to the rescue when the bat sign shines in the sky; God: comes to the rescue when his people pray

❀ Wonder Woman: has a magic truth lasso; God: offers the truth through the Bible and through his Son, Jesus.

We try to know more about God by comparing him to things that we understand. In a power contest between the school principal and God, God wins by a mile! If you added all the power of the president plus all the power of Superman and Batman, God would still have more power!

The Bible gives many examples of God's amazing power.

Genesis 1:1–3 says,

"In the beginning God created the sky and the earth. The earth was empty and had no form. Darkness covered the ocean, and God's Spirit was moving over the water. Then God said, 'Let there be light,' and there was light."

God is so powerful, he created light for the whole world with just his words. That was the first day of creation. Then God went on to create the rest of the world and everything in it. Only God can create like that! If you have ever tried to will something to happen—like making the red traffic light change, or getting your homework to do itself—you probably understand more clearly that the power to create a world, a universe, or a tree belongs to God alone. When you think of God, the Creator, you get some sense of how awesome his power really is.

Power-up with more examples of God's power from the Bible.

1. *Power over nature (Joshua 4:23–24)*
2. *Power over armies (Isaiah 37:14–36)*
3. *Power over death (John 11:38–44)*

Just as God's power created everything, his great power continues to sustain all of creation. That means God keeps the world going. God makes the world turn and the seasons change. He makes it possible for bodies to heal and imaginations to think of new things. God answers prayers, heals broken hearts, and guides our lives. That is incredible power!

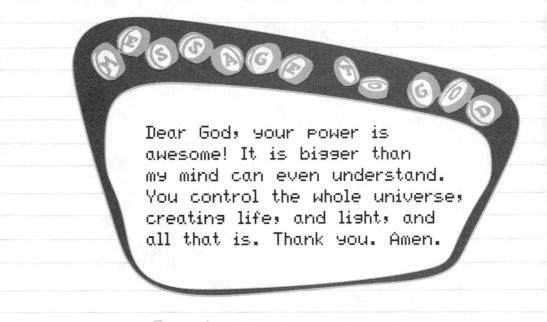

MESSAGE TO GOD

Dear God, your power is awesome! It is bigger than my mind can even understand. You control the whole universe, creating life, and light, and all that is. Thank you. Amen.

Prayer Starters

God, here are three things that I think show your power...

God, I need your power to help me with...

God, thanks for your healing power for . . .

 God, today I'm thinking about all the things you created: the hillsides, the mountains, the rivers, and me. I am in awe of your power. Amen.

Here's what I think about God's power . . .

I'm so glad God has power because . . .

I saw the news on September 11, 2001. Seeing the two World Trade Center towers fall apart was really scary. I thought for a long time about all those people in the airplanes and in the towers. Sometimes in Sunday school we sing "He's Got the Whole World in His Hands." Did God have all those people in his hands that day?

signed,
Kinda' Scared

MESSAGE TO GOD

Lord, I don't understand why so many sad things happen in the world. It seems like something bad happens every day. Do you really have us in your hands? Amen.

God's hOldiNg YOU in hIs hAnDs

- ❀ *He always hears your prayers.*
- ❀ *He knows your heart.*
- ❀ *He heals you with forgiveness.*
- ❀ *He helps you through each day.*
- ❀ *He holds you every moment.*

15

We know from the Bible that God is in control of everything. Yes! God really does hold each of us in his hand. The Bible also tells us that God is good. Because God is good, he doesn't want bad things (like the tragedy of September 11) to happen. So why *do* bad things happen?

God gives every person something called "free will." That means people are free to make their own choices. Some people choose greed, hatred, and sin instead of the good things God wants for them. When people choose sin, bad things—even deaths—happen. Sometimes these bad things happen to Christians. Even then, God gives his people a special promise.

Romans 8:37–39 says,

"But in all these things we have full victory through God who showed his love for us. Yes, I am sure that neither death, nor life, nor angels, nor ruling spirits, nothing now, nothing in the future, no powers, nothing above us, nothing below us, nor anything else in the whole world will ever be able to separate us from the love of God that is in Christ Jesus our Lord."

Do these verses help you see how much God loves you? He will never let anything get in the way of that love. God holds you in his hands every single day.

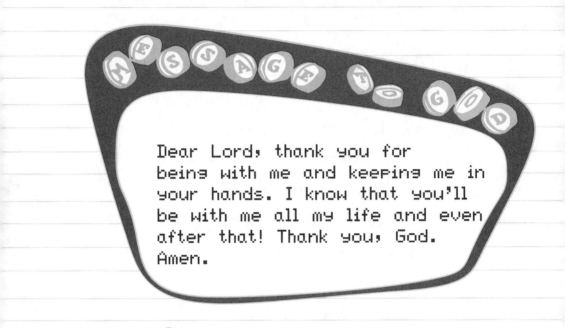

MESSAGE TO GOD

Dear Lord, thank you for being with me and keeping me in your hands. I know that you'll be with me all my life and even after that! Thank you, God. Amen.

Prayer Starters

Lord, I pray for the people in …

Lord, even though I know your special promise, I feel afraid that …

Lord, I want to choose the good things you want
for me. Help me with . . .

Lord, I still believe you have the
whole world in your hands, and I'm
grateful for that. Thank you for
watching over me. Amen.

Here's what God showed me in his Word that assures me
he is in control . . .

God answered my prayer this way . . .

God's promise helps me feel safer because . . .

My pastor at church says that God is holy and we're supposed to be, too. What does that mean? Whatever it means, I know I'm not doing it right because I keep messing up. The other day I lost my homework, so I copied it from a friend. I know that was wrong. I think if I'm supposed to be holy, I need some help!

signed,
Struggling

MESSAGE TO GOD

Dear God, I know I do things you don't like. I try to be holy like you, but I really need your help in doing right things. How can I be holy? Amen.

What's it like to be HoLy?

- ❁ Be compassionate.
- ❁ Be kind.
- ❁ Be humble.
- ❁ Be gentle.
- ❁ Be patient.

The word *holy* means pure, perfect, and separate. Things in the world don't fit that description! By contrast, God is holy. That means he is perfect and totally separate from anything that isn't pure.

Because Christians are God's children, we are supposed to show other people what God is like. That's why we are called to be holy.

1 Peter 1:15, 16 says,
"Be holy in all you do, just as God, the One who called you, is holy. It is written in the Scriptures: 'You must be holy, because I am holy.'"

When we are living holy lives, people around us will see the difference. The Bible tells us how very beautiful lives lived in holiness can be.

Colossians 3:12–13 says,

"God has chosen you and made you his holy people. He loves you. So always do these things: show mercy to others, be kind, humble, gentle, and patient. Get along with each other, and forgive each other."

Of course, holiness is not something we are able to achieve on our own. If we try to be perfect, even for an hour, we find out how much we need help! The Holy Spirit living in us makes us able to live holy lives. Our job is to listen to the Holy Spirit. For example, if you have to choose between copying a friend's homework or getting in trouble, listen for the Holy Spirit. He will be nudging you toward the right choice.

The more you study your Bible to find out what's right, and the more you listen for the Holy Spirit's voice in you, the more you will be able to live a holy life. Pray that God will help you be holy. Pray and ask him to help you hear the Holy Spirit.

MESSAGE TO GOD

Lord, I can try harder to please you. Thank you for the Holy Spirit who helps me be holy. Amen.

Prayer Starters

Lord, I need help with being more patient with . . .

God, help me listen to the Holy Spirit about this choice . . .

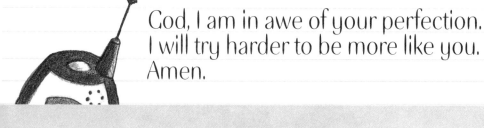

God, I am in awe of your perfection. I will try harder to be more like you. Amen.

One way I can try to be more holy is by . . .

This is how I feel when I've acted in a way that's not right . . .

Even though I've known about Jesus since I was a little kid, I still don't feel sure about who he is. Sometimes I think of him as God's Son, and sometimes as the baby in a manger, and sometimes as the one who died on the cross. Some friends at school say Jesus was just a teacher, but I learned in Sunday school that Jesus is God. I'm not sure now. Is Jesus God?

signed,

Jesus' Friend

MESSAGE TO GOD

Dear God, I thought up till now I knew who Jesus was, but I wonder if you can help me understand more about him. Thanks. Amen.

JeSUs' MaNy NamEs

- ❀ Messiah
- ❀ Son of God
- ❀ Prince of Peace
- ❀ Alpha and Omega (the first and the last)

Though Jesus was a great teacher, and other great teachers have lived, Jesus is the only one who died for our sins and then rose again from the dead. Is Jesus God? The short answer is yes! Jesus is the baby in the manger *and* the man who died on the cross. Jesus is God's Son. He's all of the above.

God is one. But God has presented himself to us in three persons: God the Father; Jesus, God's Son; and the Holy Spirit. Just *how* God does this is a mystery to humans, but we know it's true because the Bible tells us! Jesus is God.

Check out these Bible verses that tell us Jesus is God.
1. John 1:1–18
2. Matthew 16:15–17
3. John 10:30

God's three persons—including Jesus—are part of God's wonderful plan for loving and saving people.

John 3:16, 17 says,
"God loved the world so much that he gave his one and only Son so that whoever believes in him may not be lost, but have eternal life. God did not send his Son into the world to judge the world guilty, but to save the world through him."

God's plan for you (and for everybody) is that you would live happily with God for eternity. The work Jesus did when he came to earth makes that possible. You may have been hearing that Jesus loves you since you were just a little kid. Now you can see how important that is.

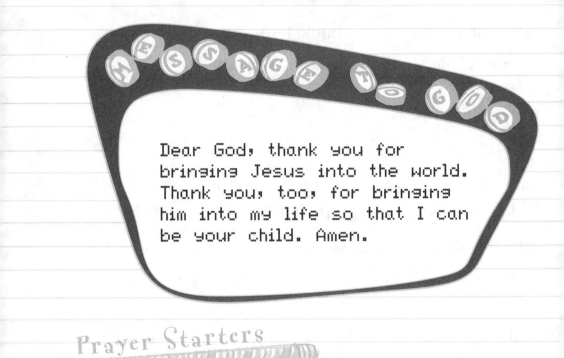

MESSAGE TO GOD

Dear God, thank you for bringing Jesus into the world. Thank you, too, for bringing him into my life so that I can be your child. Amen.

Prayer Starters

Dear God, help me understand . . .

Dear God, thank you for Jesus . . .

God, I'm still struggling with . . .

Dear Jesus, I will always be glad to have your love and to share your love with others. I know that you are God. Amen.

I know that Jesus is God because . . .

My life is blessed by Jesus because . . .

I am thankful to Jesus for . . .

We don't really pray that much at my house. Sometimes we say grace before dinner, but that's about it. My mom has prayed for me when I was sick or had a problem, but I haven't really done much of it myself. I'm not sure how to pray. How do I start? Is there a right way or a wrong way to pray?

signed,

Need to Pray

MESSAGE TO GOD

Dear God, please teach me how to pray so that I can really talk to you from my heart. Thank you. Amen.

four P's to Prayer

❀ *Prepare—Pick a quiet time when you can talk to God.*

❀ *Plan—Make a list of things you want to talk to God about.*

❀ *Praise—Tell God how great you think he is. Give God thanks.*

❀ *Petition—Ask God for help.*

Prayer is so important to your relationship with God. Jesus understood you might have questions about it, so when he was on earth, he gave instructions about prayer. You can read some of them in Matthew 6.

Jesus also gave an example that we can follow when we pray.

Matthew 6:9–13 says,

"Our Father in heaven, may your name always be kept holy. May your kingdom come and what you want be done, here on earth as it is in heaven. Give us the food we need for each day. Forgive us for our sins, just as we have forgiven those who sinned against us. And do not cause us to be tempted, but save us from the Evil One."

Jesus' example prayer is sometimes called the "Lord's Prayer." A lot of people memorize it so they can say it anytime. The Lord's Prayer is a good guide for any other prayers you want to say. In the Lord's Prayer, Jesus shows how to address God with respect and reverence. He shows us how to ask for things that we need—including forgiveness for our sins and help to stay away from temptation. Try saying the Lord's Prayer with your own name in place of *us* or *we*.

Follow Jesus' example when you pray. Other than that, there is no wrong way to pray, and no wrong time. You can pray while you're on the school bus, in the shower, alone in your room, or on your bike. You don't always have to bow your head and fold your hands, either. You can try praying with your hands lifted up or try singing a prayer. Find out which ways help you make the best connection to God.

MESSAGE TO GOD

Dear Father in heaven, thank you for showing me how to pray. Help me to remember the Lord's Prayer and to share my heart with you. Thank you, God. Amen.

Prayer Starters

Help me, God, to find the best time and place to pray. I think I might try praying like this . . .

God, here's what the Lord's Prayer sounds like in my own words . . .

Dear God, thank you for helping me learn to pray better. I'm going to keep practicing and trying to get closer to you. Amen.

I found that the best place for me to pray is . . .

Here's a list of things I'm praying about . . .

Thank you, God, for hearing my prayer about . . .

When I was at camp, we went around in a circle praying about something we're thankful for. Well, it wasn't hard for me to think of something, but it was hard to pray out loud. I just gave a quick, one-word answer. Some kids really said nice prayers, though. I'm too nervous to pray out loud. Is there a way to get over that?

signed,

Speechless

MESSAGE TO GOD

Dear God, please help me feel better about praying out loud. I don't even like to do it at home at the dinner table. Amen.

TuRn uP tHe VoluMe

🌼 Pray aloud when you're alone.

🌼 Practice with a small tape recorder so you can hear your own voice.

🌼 Pray with just one friend until you're really comfortable.

🌼 Write down your prayer first and then read it to a group that you want to pray with.

You're not the only person who feels nervous about praying out loud. Even adults worry about it sometimes. That's pretty natural. But don't let your shyness stop you from praying with your fellow Christians. The Bible tells us how powerful it is when Christians share their prayers.

Matthew 18:19, 20 says,

"Also, I tell you that if two of you on earth agree about something and pray for it, it will be done for you by my Father in heaven. This is true because if two or three people come together in my name, I am there with them."

Your shyness about praying out loud may come from a fear that you won't say exactly the right thing. Maybe you're afraid the prayer won't come out just as you meant it. If that's your fear, keep in mind that your effort to share from your heart is more important than how your words sound. God's not interested in big, fluffy words. He just wants to hear from you. So relax!

People who are able to pray anytime and anywhere are sometimes called "prayer warriors." Prayer warriors are great because they know prayer can help change things. You can be a prayer warrior, too. You get better at anything when you practice, and prayer is no exception. Even when you're alone, practice saying prayers out loud.

Learning to pray aloud is a matter of feeling free to share your heart. Then it's a matter of practice.

Praying with others can make a big difference in your life, so don't be too nervous to do it!

MESSAGE TO GOD

Lord, please help me keep my mind on you so I'm more at ease when I pray out loud. Help me to remember that I don't have to talk a lot, I just have to share my heart with you. Amen.

Prayer Starters

Lord, help me to pray out loud with ...

Dear God, here is a prayer I will pray out loud next time I'm in a prayer group ...

Lord, please give me the courage to practice praying . . .

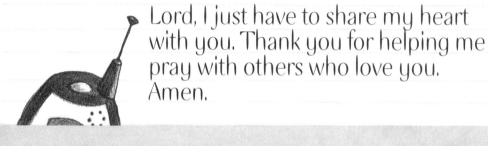

Lord, I just have to share my heart with you. Thank you for helping me pray with others who love you. Amen.

I'm practicing praying out loud with . . .

God is helping me to learn to pray out loud by . . .

I am practicing this little prayer out loud . . .

Sometimes I wonder if my prayers make a difference. I've prayed for friends and my family, but I don't know if God heard me since I'm just a kid. Sometimes I even try to pray for the president. I pray for my dog, too. I don't know. Do a kid's prayers really matter?

signed,

Just a Kid

MESSAGE TO GOD

God, I am sure you're very busy. If you have time to hear this prayer, could you show me a little more about how it all works? Thanks. Amen.

rEasoNs to tAlk to God

- ❀ To know God better.
- ❀ To ask for help when you don't know what to do.
- ❀ To thank God for good things.
- ❀ To share your heart.
- ❀ To express love for God.

Philippians 4:6, 7 says,
"Do not worry about anything, but pray and ask God for everything you need, always giving thanks. And God's peace, which is so great we cannot understand it, will keep your hearts and minds in Christ Jesus."

This verse tells you to pray and ask for whatever you want or need. This verse is speaking to kids, too! The Bible doesn't say you have to be an adult if you want to pray. It doesn't say you have to be a minister or have a diploma of some kind to get God's attention.

Prayer is your direct link to God.

God wants his people to talk to him, every day, and all the time—that means you, too!

The prayers of ministers, moms and dads, and even little children all go immediately to God. God knows the strength that can come from kids who truly follow him. Your prayers make a difference. God listens each time you call on him.

Check out the stories of these young people who talked to God.
1. David
2. Samuel
3. Timothy

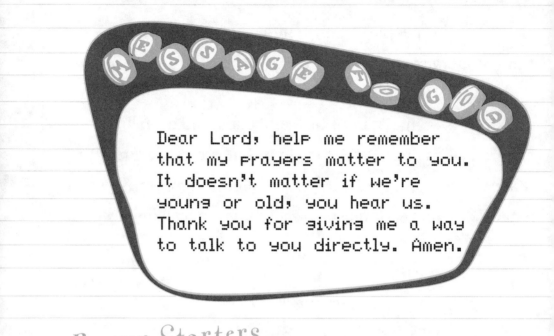

MESSAGE TO GOD

Dear Lord, help me remember that my prayers matter to you. It doesn't matter if we're young or old, you hear us. Thank you for giving me a way to talk to you directly. Amen.

Prayer Starters

God, today I'm praying for...

Lord, please hear my prayer about...

Thanks, God, for hearing my prayer for . . .

God, I believe you hear every prayer. I know that in your time, you will answer my prayers. Thank you, God. Amen.

This is what happened when I prayed for . . .

I have been praying for . . .

I believe that God hears my prayers because . . .

49

I prayed that my dad would get a new job. I prayed for his job to be in our city so we wouldn't have to move. A few days later, my dad told me he was taking a job in another state. I couldn't decide if that was God answering part of my prayer, but not the rest, or what? Is there any way to understand God's answers to prayer?

signed,

Need an Answer

MESSAGE TO GOD

God, I don't know how to tell if you're answering my prayers. Do you sometimes answer part of a prayer but not the whole thing? Can you help me with this? Amen.

poSsibLe anSweRs to pRayEr

- ❀ Yes.
- ❀ No.
- ❀ Maybe.
- ❀ Ask again later.
- ❀ I've got a better idea.

Psalm 145:17-19 says,
*"Everything the Lord does is right. He is loyal to all he
has made. The Lord is close to everyone who prays to
him, to all who truly pray to him. He gives those who
respect him what they want. He listens when they cry,
and he saves them."*

God always answers your prayers. God listens to your prayers,
and because he loves you, he answers according to what is
right. There's never a time when God is not interested in what
you have to say.

Sometimes we think God hasn't answered our prayers because
he did not give us what we told him we wanted. Sometimes
when we pray, we already have an answer in our minds that
we hope God will go for. Sometimes we are so determined
about what we want God's answer to be, it seems like we pray
just to see if God will agree with us.

If you're hoping to find a Bible verse that says God always answers my prayers *the way I want him to,* then you're going to be disappointed. There's no secret formula that says just plug in these words, stir three times, and wait five minutes, then the answer will come out like this. Your prayers are not like rubbing the lamp of a genie and getting three magic wishes. Instead of trying to make God agree with you, ask God for his will to be done in your life. God knows your needs and your heart. Trust him to take care of you.

If you still need help recognizing God's answers to your prayers, keep a prayer journal, like the one in this book! Write down what you pray for. Then follow up by writing down what happened as a result.

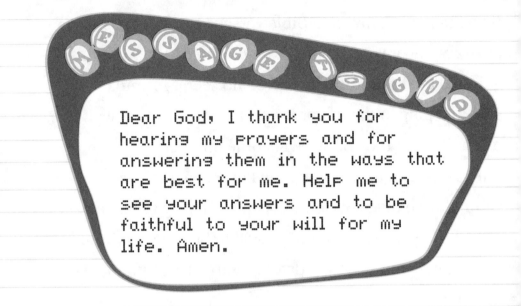

MESSAGE TO GOD

Dear God, I thank you for hearing my prayers and for answering them in the ways that are best for me. Help me to see your answers and to be faithful to your will for my life. Amen.

Prayer Starters

Lord, thanks for saying *no* to my prayer about …

Dear God, show me your answer to my prayer for …

Thank you, Lord, for listening to all my prayers. I trust you to guide my life. Amen.

God answered the prayer for . . .

When God said *no* to my prayer, I . . .

One way I've learned to trust God's answers is by . . .

My grandmother died recently and one of the old things we found at her house was a big family Bible. My mom was so excited to have it because it's a special book. Even though I have a newer Bible at home, I couldn't help thinking about how very old the Bible really is. I was wondering if it could really mean all that much to read a book that's so old. Does the Bible really have meaning today?

signed,

Young Bible-Reader

MESSAGE TO GOD

Dear God, please help me understand why it's important to read the Bible. Can't I get as much by reading some other book about you? Amen.

fUn BibLe faCts

- ❀ The Old Testament is made up of 39 books.

- ❀ The New Testament is made up of 27 books.

- ❀ The Bible was originally written in Aramaic, Hebrew, and Greek.

- ❀ The Bible was written over a span of about 1500 years.

It's true that the Bible was written a long time ago. In fact, parts of the Old Testament were written over 3000 years ago! But the Bible has stood the test of time. Why do people still read it?

One reason that the Bible still matters to people today is the fact that it's mainly a book about love. It is the greatest love story the world has ever seen—the story of God's love for his people. God's love story has strong heroes and amazing miracles, too. That kind of story never gets old!

Another reason the Bible is important even after so many years is because God guides readers of every generation as they study his Word. God wants everyone in every era of history to know about Jesus, the Savior. The Bible also tells God's people how he wants them to live their lives.

2 Timothy 3:16, 17 says,

"All Scripture is given by God and is useful for teaching, for showing people what is wrong in their lives, for correcting faults, and for teaching how to live right. Using the Scriptures, the person who serves God will be capable, having all that is needed to do every good work."

Wow! Those are great verses! God's Word is such a blessing. Be glad that God loves you so much that he provided this wonderful tool for you to get to know him even better. Let the Bible lead you and teach you.

God wants everyone in every era of history to know about Jesus, the Savior.

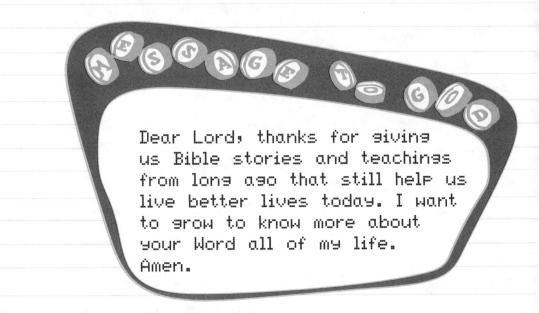

MESSAGE TO GOD

Dear Lord, thanks for giving us Bible stories and teachings from long ago that still help us live better lives today. I want to grow to know more about your Word all of my life. Amen.

Prayer Starters

God, here are the verses I'm reading today . . .

Thanks, God for giving us your Word. My favorite part of the Bible is . . .

Help me find ways to understand more about this verse . . .

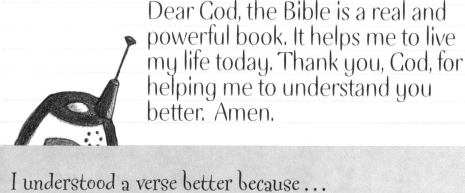

Dear God, the Bible is a real and powerful book. It helps me to live my life today. Thank you, God, for helping me to understand you better. Amen.

I understood a verse better because . . .

God helped me see more clearly about . . .

I think the Bible is still a great book because . . .

Last Christmas, my aunt gave me a teen study Bible and said that she hoped it would help me study God's Word more. The truth is I haven't read it at all. I know the basic Bible stories, but I don't really know where to find them or how to get started. It's just overwhelming. Is there an easy way to get into it?

signed,

Challenged to Study

MESSAGE TO GOD

Hi, God. I want to read your stories in the Bible, but I don't exactly know how to get going with it. Please help me find a good way to study the Bible. Amen.

Good ways to eXploRe

❀ See if your Bible has a reading plan. The plan will tell you what to read each day.

❀ Start with one of the Gospels. Those first four books of the New Testament tell the stories of Jesus.

❀ Ask your friends if they have a favorite book of the Bible. Start there.

Treat your Bible like a treasure chest you are about to open. Even though it takes hard work, Bible study will help you live the way God wants you to live. Answers you'll find in the Bible are like valuable nuggets of gold.

2 Peter 3:17, 18 says,
"Be careful so you will not fall from your strong faith. But grow in the grace and knowledge of our Lord and Savior Jesus Christ."

There are lots of ways to study the Bible. The best thing is to just get started. Read the passage you've chosen several times. If you get confused, stop. Write down the questions you have about the passage and then leave that section and explore another. You can come back later and try to find the answer to your question, or ask another Christian about it.

If you have friends that are interested in learning more about the Bible, you can form a group and read it together. Christian bookstores have study guides that your group can follow. Or ask a mature Christian teen to help guide your group.

Whether you're learning in a group or studying on your own, pray for God to help you with your Bible readings. Ask him to give you understanding.

God's Word is your way to become all that he wants you to become, so search each part with an open and loving heart.

Lord, thank you for your Word. Thank you that I have a Bible to read that's just for kids. Please help me get started and keep going with it so I can know more about you. Amen.

Prayer Starters

God, today I'm starting by reading the book of...

Lord, please give me a greater desire to read your Word. I want to read about...

Lord, thank you for this verse because . . .

Lord, I am learning to read the Bible. I am happy that I have your wonderful book to help me live a better life. Amen.

God showed me a truth in this verse . . .

I can use what I learned by reading God's Word when I . . .

Here's where I started reading . . .

I admit that I don't think it's fun to read the Bible. I try to read it, but I really don't get it. It's the same way I feel at church sometimes. My mind drifts when I'm supposed to be listening to the sermons. Is there a way to make the Bible stuff easier to understand? I just feel so dumb!

signed,

Fumbling Along

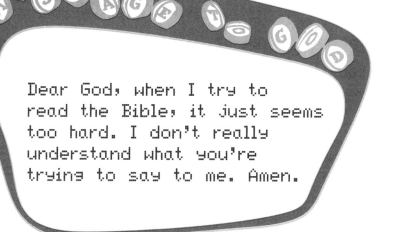

MESSAGE TO GOD

Dear God, when I try to read the Bible, it just seems too hard. I don't really understand what you're trying to say to me. Amen.

tIps for BibLe study

✿ *Loosen up—Relax and ask the Holy Spirit to guide you.*

✿ *Lift up—Pray for God to help you understand.*

✿ *Listen up—Read a passage out loud.*

✿ *Look up—Use a good dictionary to define hard words.*

2 Timothy 3:15 says,
"Since you were a child you have known the Holy Scriptures which are able to make you wise. And that wisdom leads to salvation through faith in Christ Jesus."

The Bible is a book that makes you think. You have to be willing to take some time to study and understand it. Wise King Solomon gives us a clue in Proverbs.

Proverbs 1:7 says,
"Knowledge begins with respect for the Lord."

Solomon knew what he was talking about! He became the wisest man ever to live. Do you know how? He asked God for wisdom. That's what you should do, too. Whenever you're about to read God's Word, or listen to God's message in church, pray for the Holy Spirit to help you understand. God wants us to read his Word. He wants us to be wise. He will be very glad to help you!

God wants you to learn more about him through his Word so you can live a better life—the way God wants you to live. God's Word helps you make smarter choices every day. Don't be afraid of the challenge of understanding God's Word. Give it a chance. Give yourself a chance. The Holy Spirit will find a way to help you understand.

Whenever you're about to read God's Word, or listen to God's message in church, pray for the Holy Spirit to help you understand.

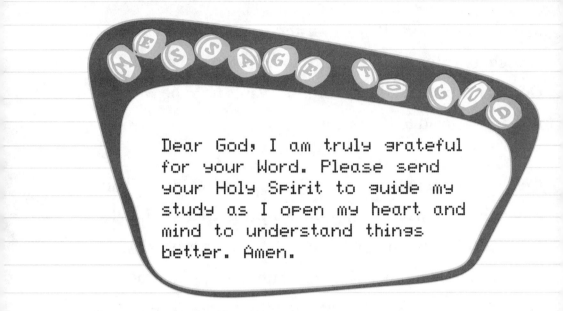

MESSAGE TO GOD

Dear God, I am truly grateful for your Word. Please send your Holy Spirit to guide my study as I open my heart and mind to understand things better. Amen.

Prayer Starters

Lord, help me understand what you want me to know about this topic . . .

Lord, thank you for helping me understand this verse . . .

Thanks, God, for letting me take this one little step at a time. Today I read . . .

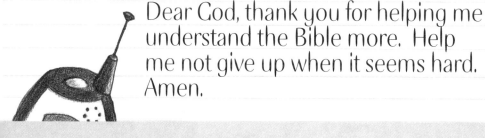

Dear God, thank you for helping me understand the Bible more. Help me not give up when it seems hard. Amen.

Here's what I understand about this verse . . .

I talked to my friend about a verse, and we agreed that it means . . .

I am taking _____ minutes a day to read my Bible. It's a big help because . . .

I like mysteries! I read detective books—even the *Hardy Boys* that my dad used to read. I like mystery movies and *Scooby-Doo*. Mom says some problems in life are like mysteries, but we can always get help solving them from God's Word. When things in my life feel like a mystery, can the Bible really help?

signed,

Clueless

Lord, I know you have all the answers. So many things in my life feel like a mystery to me. Can your Word help clear things up? Amen.

bE a BiBle dEtectiVe

❀ Tell God about your mystery through prayer.

❀ Find Bible verses that talk about your mystery.

❀ Be at peace. You've turned the mystery over to God.

Sometimes God speaks to his people in mysterious ways. However, more often, God gives us answers very plainly in his Word. God's Word can help you with every concern that life may bring. Christians have used it for centuries as a guide for making decisions and solving problems of every kind.

2 Timothy 3:17 says,
"Using the Scriptures, the person who serves God will be capable, having all that is needed to do every good work."

Here's how to find "clues" in God's Word to help you solve any mystery (or problem) you may have. After you send your problem to God through prayer, next find Bible verses or stories that relate. Use the glossary or concordance in the back of your Bible to find as many passages as possible.

Now pray again. This time ask God to help you figure out what the Bible verses mean. He will help you figure out what to do.

The Bible can solve these mysteries.
What should I do . . .
   Mystery 1. When I feel afraid: Joshua 1:9
   Mystery 2. When someone hurts me: Luke 6:27–31
   Mystery 3. When I'm angry: James 1:19, 20

Do you see in each of those examples how the Bible helped? Try a few of your own and see what help you find.

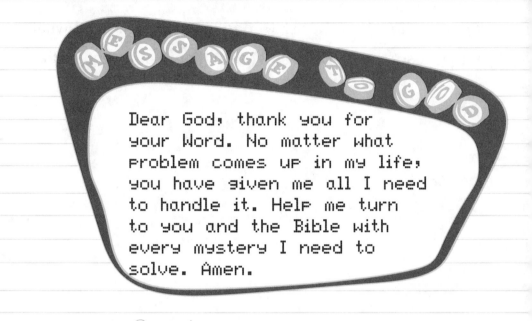

MESSAGE TO GOD

Dear God, thank you for your Word. No matter what problem comes up in my life, you have given me all I need to handle it. Help me turn to you and the Bible with every mystery I need to solve. Amen.

Prayer Starters

God, thanks for helping me understand . . .

Lord, thanks for showing me how to solve problems by reading your Word. I trust your Word. Amen.

God showed me this verse _____ to help me with . . .

God helped me see things differently about . . .

I memorized this verse to help me with . . .

My dad took my family to New York City. I have never been to such a huge city before, and it was amazing to see so many different people. I wondered how God could take care of them all. And I wondered if God knew I was in the middle of New York City. Can he really care about me when he has so many different people to watch over?

signed,

One Kid in a Million

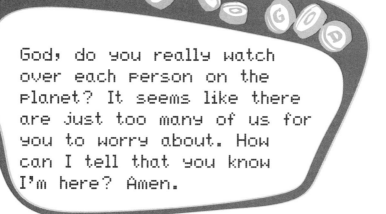

God, do you really watch over each person on the planet? It seems like there are just too many of us for you to worry about. How can I tell that you know I'm here? Amen.

God kNowS alL aBouT yOu

- ❀ He knows how many hairs are on your head.

- ❀ He knows what makes you laugh.

- ❀ He knows your shoe size and your favorite T-shirt.

- ❀ He knows your heart.

The world is full of people. Each one of them is different, yet God knows all about every person he created. Each one is important to God. That means you, too! It's pretty awesome to realize that the God who created the whole universe knows all about you. Think about old friends that you've known and loved forever. God knows you and loves you even more than that.

Don't be worried that there are too many people in the world for God to take care of. God has enough power to do it. And God knows everything, too, so he never loses track of his people.

In Psalm 23, the Bible tells about God's love and concern for you. You may already know this one well. A lot of people memorize it because it is a great reminder of God's faithfulness to us. That's very comforting.

Psalm 23 says,

"The Lord is my shepherd; I have everything I need. He lets me rest in green pastures. He leads me to calm water. He gives me new strength. He leads me on paths that are right for the good of his name. Even if I walk through a very dark valley, I will not be afraid, because you are with me. Your rod and your walking stick comfort me. You prepare a meal for me in front of my enemies. You pour oil on my head; you fill my cup to overflowing. Surely your goodness and love will be with me all my life, and I will live in the house of the Lord forever."

Try reading that again. This time, use your own name instead of *my* or *I.*

Just as a shepherd takes care of the needs of his sheep, God takes care of his people.

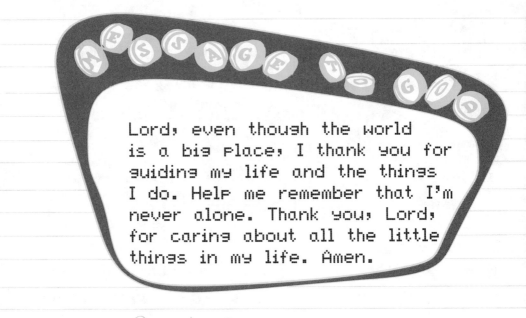

MESSAGE TO GOD

Lord, even though the world is a big place, I thank you for guiding my life and the things I do. Help me remember that I'm never alone. Thank you, Lord, for caring about all the little things in my life. Amen.

Prayer Starters

Lord, thank you for caring about . . .

Dear God, please help me with this . . .

Lord, thank you for showing me all the
ways that you really care about me.
Amen.

This week, I knew God cared for me because . . .

I have learned to trust that God cares for me because . . .

My youth group did this activity about faith and trust. We took turns falling backwards and trusting that the rest of the group would catch us. When it was my turn, I wondered if my friends would catch me or not. Our youth leader said the activity was like trusting in God. She said it takes faith to trust God. Is that really what faith is about?

signed,

Trying to Trust

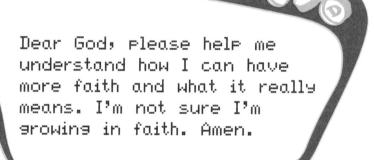

MESSAGE TO GOD

Dear God, please help me understand how I can have more faith and what it really means. I'm not sure I'm growing in faith. Amen.

wHat do yOu hAve fAitH iN?

- ❀ Faith that the chair will hold you
- ❀ Faith that spring will come
- ❀ Faith that chocolate ice cream will always be good

In our everyday lives, we have faith in simple things. You need faith in yourself to speak in front of a group. You have faith in the airline pilots when you go up in an airplane. These everyday things give just a glimpse of what it means to have faith in God.

The Bible gives God's definition of faith.

Hebrews 11:1–3 says,
"Faith means being sure of the things we hope for and knowing that something is real even if we do not see it. Faith is the reason we remember great people who lived in the past. It is by faith we understand that the whole world was made by God's command so what we see was made by something that cannot be seen."

Placing your faith in God is a lot bigger than having faith that a chair will hold you up when you sit on it. But look at the amazing rewards godly faith can bring! Noah's faith saved him from the flood and Moses' faith helped a whole nation escape from slavery. Look up and read all of Hebrews 11 to see more examples of those who have gone before you who showed great faith in God.

So what kind of faith does God want you to show in your life? We need to have enough faith in God, to trust his plan for us. That means we should always do what he wants us to do—even if we can't see how it will turn out in the end. We can show faith in God by not worrying about problems. Instead, pray and tell God about your problems. Then trust him to help you get through them.

Hebrews 11:6 says,
"Without faith no one can please God. Anyone who comes to God must believe that he is real and that he rewards those who truly want to find him."

God really wants to take care of you. He will be good to you. Placing your faith in God will lead to great rewards. One of the rewards is you don't have to be stressed out by your problems—you know God is dealing with them.

MESSAGE TO GOD

Lord, I believe. I have faith that you hear and answer my prayers according to what's best for me. Help me trust you in all the things I do. Thank you for helping my faith grow. Amen.

Prayer Starters

Lord, I believe in you. Please help me have faith in . . .

Lord, I know my faith is weak. I need help with . . .

God, please help me to trust you with this problem . . .

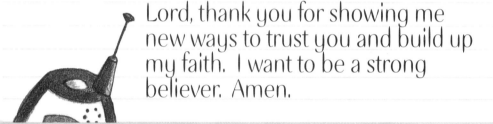

Lord, thank you for showing me new ways to trust you and build up my faith. I want to be a strong believer. Amen.

God helped me understand faith better by . . .

I learned this Bible verse about faith . . .

I believe in God, but sometimes I start to wonder if he's real. I hate to admit it, but I have so many questions. I don't know if other kids feel that way. If they do, nobody talks about it. These feelings of doubt make me feel terrible! How can I get rid of them? What should I do?

signed,

Questioning

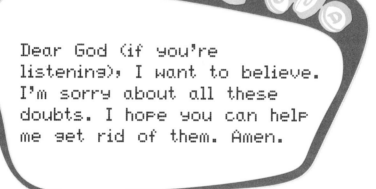

MESSAGE TO GOD

Dear God (if you're listening), I want to believe. I'm sorry about all these doubts. I hope you can help me get rid of them. Amen.

tHe dOuBt DiaRiEs

- ✿ Moses doubted he could talk to Pharaoh, but believed God and delivered the message.

- ✿ Gideon didn't let his doubt pull the "wool" over his eyes.

- ✿ John the Baptist doubted whether he was truly meant to baptize Jesus.

Doubt is not a new thing. It is part of the walk of nearly every believer. Just look at the story of "doubting Thomas." Thomas needed proof before he would believe that Jesus had come back to life. He wanted to touch Jesus and see the scars in Jesus' hands. Thomas was struggling with doubt. Then Jesus helped Thomas to overcome his doubt. If we share our feelings of doubt with the Lord, he will help us, too.

God wants you to share with him about everything in your life—including your doubt. God is not a God of confusion. When you give your doubts and questions to God, he will help you understand more clearly.

In our prayers to overcome doubt, we can use the words of the boy's father in Mark 9.

Mark 9:24 says,
"Immediately the father cried out, 'I do believe!
Help me to believe more!'"

God answers our prayer for more faith because he wants to strengthen our spirits and help us to grow closer to him. Just as Jesus helped Thomas believe, he helps us believe, too.

It's better to believe than to doubt. However, many believers experience doubt.

Don't let doubt keep you down. Instead, ask God to help you believe the truth.

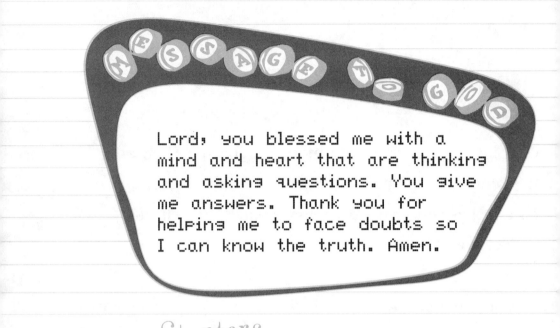

MESSAGE TO GOD

Lord, you blessed me with a mind and heart that are thinking and asking questions. You give me answers. Thank you for helping me to face doubts so I can know the truth. Amen.

Prayer Starters

God, I really have doubts about…

Lord, I can't help wondering if it's true that…

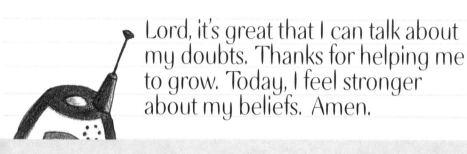

Lord, it's great that I can talk about my doubts. Thanks for helping me to grow. Today, I feel stronger about my beliefs. Amen.

God helped clear my doubts by . . .

This Bible verse helped me see God's truth . . .

I am learning to trust God more about . . .

My friends and I have done a couple of really dumb things lately, like taking candy from stores or making goofy prank calls. At first I thought it was funny, but then I started feeling really bad. How can I keep from doing stupid stuff like this?

signed,
Tempted Again

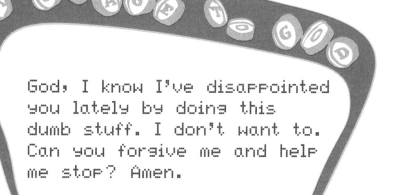

MESSAGE TO GOD

God, I know I've disappointed you lately by doing this dumb stuff. I don't want to. Can you forgive me and help me stop? Amen.

wHo Did RiGht?

See how these people from the Bible dealt with temptation.

- ❀ Eve: Genesis 3:1–6
- ❀ Joseph: Genesis 39:6–12
- ❀ Jesus: Matthew 4:1–11

Matthew 26:41 says,
"Stay awake and pray for strength against temptation. The spirit wants to do what is right, but the body is weak."

God recognizes that it's not always easy to do right. We have choices to make every day. It is hard to say *no* to fun or funny things that your friends are doing—even though you know they're wrong. God will forgive you when you make a mistake, but he has a better plan for your life.

1 Corinthians 10:13 says,
"You can trust God, who will not permit you to be tempted more than you can stand. But when you are tempted, he will also give you a way to escape so that you will be able to stand it."

God promises to help you when you face temptations. He promises that there will always be a way out of a tempting situation. Your job is to take the escape route. **Run** away from the thing that's tempting you!

Prepare for temptation before it happens!
1. Make a list of things that tempt you.
2. Memorize Bible verses that can answer the temptation.
3. Ask God's help to make you stronger than the temptation.
4. Stay away from things that tempt you.

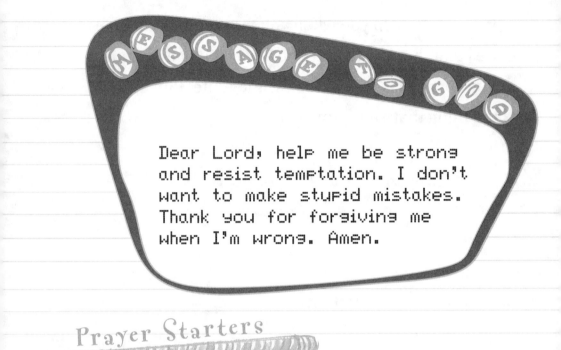

MESSAGE TO GOD

Dear Lord, help me be strong and resist temptation. I don't want to make stupid mistakes. Thank you for forgiving me when I'm wrong. Amen.

Prayer Starters

God, I really blew it this time . . .

God, I'm so tempted to . . .

God, here's my plan for facing a temptation . . .

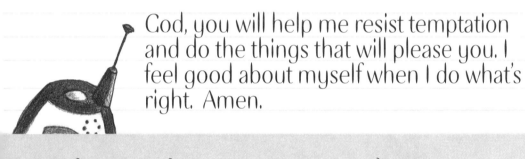

God, you will help me resist temptation and do the things that will please you. I feel good about myself when I do what's right. Amen.

God is showing me how to resist temptation by . . .

I resisted this temptation . . .

We're having career days at our school. Speakers come in and tell us about what they do. So far, we had a medical researcher, a bridge builder, and a ballerina. I try to imagine what I'll do when I grow up. I wonder if it really matters to God. How can I figure out what God wants me to do?

signed,

Job-Hunting

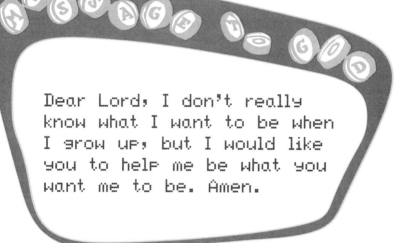

Dear Lord, I don't really know what I want to be when I grow up, but I would like you to help me be what you want me to be. Amen.

fiGuriNg oUt whAt to Do

- ✿ Make a list of things you're good at.
- ✿ Make a list of new things you'd like to try.
- ✿ Ask other Christians about their experiences.
- ✿ Listen for God's calling.

It's tough enough to figure out what you want to be, let alone what you think God wants you to be. The Bible says God wants you to be his child—no matter what career you choose.

Ephesians 4:1–3 says,
"God chose you to be his people, so I urge you now to live the life to which God called you. Always be humble, gentle, and patient, accepting each other in love. You are joined together with peace through the Spirit, so make every effort to continue together in this way."

The main job that God wants you to do is to be his child. That means choosing to be humble, gentle, patient and loving all the time—in your career and in other parts of your life. When God's people live up to this calling, then every step they take glorifies God.

Sometimes we say that someone is "called" to do a certain kind of work. A person who is called feels strongly that God wants them to do a specific job. Is God calling *you* to a certain career? It might be too soon to know. You might try several different careers before you find one that's the best for you. Pray and ask for understanding and wisdom about your career choice.

God cares about what you do now and he'll help you in the future when you're deciding about a career.

Whether you'll be a researcher or builder or minister, God asks you to do your job in a way that honors him.

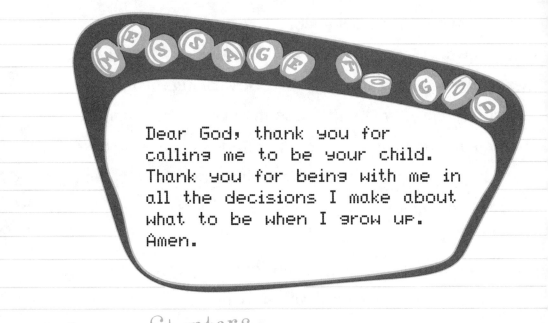

MESSAGE TO GOD

Dear God, thank you for calling me to be your child. Thank you for being with me in all the decisions I make about what to be when I grow up. Amen.

Prayer Starters

Lord, here's what I've been thinking about doing when I grow up . . .

Dear God, I have no idea what to be . . .

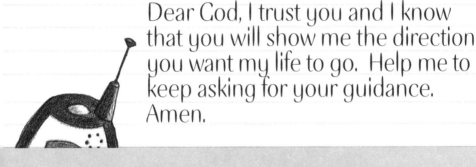

Dear God, I trust you and I know that you will show me the direction you want my life to go. Help me to keep asking for your guidance. Amen.

I don't know what I am called to be yet, but I am reading more about . . .

I know God cares about what I plan to do with my life. I believe this because . . .

You know, the New Testament in the Bible is all about God's love. Lately, I've been reading some of those Old Testament stories. Wow! There's a lot of mean stuff in there. Now I'm kind of confused between the loving God I know and the one that punished people so much. Should I be afraid?

signed,

Confused

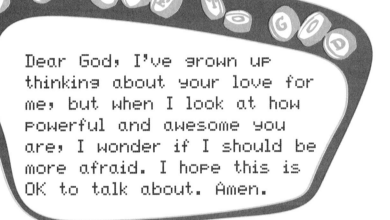

Dear God, I've grown up thinking about your love for me, but when I look at how powerful and awesome you are, I wonder if I should be more afraid. I hope this is OK to talk about. Amen.

do yOu kNow soMeonE wHo hAs...

❀ *Bibliophobia: fear of studying books*

❀ *Stinkophobia: fear of smelly socks*

❀ *Chorephobia: fear of doing housework*

When we look at some of God's stories in the Old Testament compared to the stories in the New Testament, it can feel like we're talking about two different Gods. The truth is, there's only one God. He is both terrifying and loving at the same time.

In the Old Testament and in the New Testament, God is the same.

There are reasons to fear God. God is holy and he loves justice. God is all-powerful and he will use that power to punish sin (yikes!). Because you are a believer, you know about God's power. And you know about his desire for people to stay away from sin. Believers "fear" God by having a healthy respect for his laws and his power.

Proverbs 9:10 says,
"Wisdom begins with respect for the Lord, and understanding begins with knowing the Holy One."

Believers also know that we can trust all that God does. God loves you—just like the New Testament says. That's why he sent Jesus. Through Jesus, we can have forgiveness for sins. Jesus saves us from God's punishment. Thanks to Jesus, we can feel God's love instead of hiding in fear of his punishment.

Psalm 111:7–10 says,
"Everything he does is good and fair; all his orders can be trusted. They will continue forever. They were made true and right. He sets his people free. He made his agreement everlasting. He is holy and wonderful. Wisdom begins with respect for the Lord; those who obey his orders have good understanding. He should be praised forever."

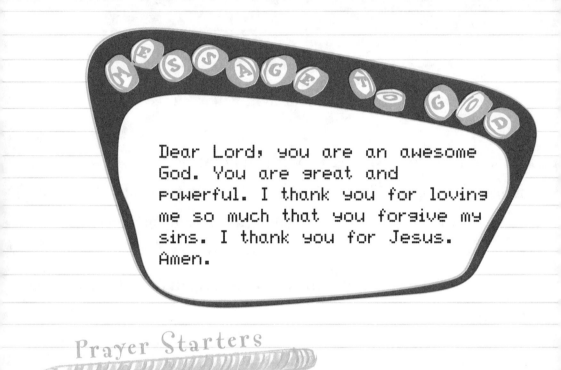

MESSAGE TO GOD

Dear Lord, you are an awesome God. You are great and powerful. I thank you for loving me so much that you forgive my sins. I thank you for Jesus. Amen.

Prayer Starters

God, today, I feel afraid because . . .

I thank you, God, for helping me with . . .

Dear God, I want to follow you always. Help me to respect and honor you all the days of my life. I praise you. Amen.

I am not afraid now because . . .

I have learned that God . . .

I will use this verse when I feel afraid . . .

I ran for president of my class. It was a pretty big deal. I put up campaign posters and made a speech. It was fun. Anyway, I lost the election. I know I'm supposed to be happy for the boy who won, but I wanted to win, too. I'm so disappointed and sad. I guess there's not much God can do when you're just blue, is there?

signed,

Blue

MESSAGE TO GOD

Lord, I'm feeling pretty
lousy about this election.
I really thought I might win.
I feel so defeated. Help me.
Amen.

tHe bLueS-bUsteRs

❀ Bake a pizza with a friend and laugh a lot.

❀ Read your Bible.

❀ Express your feelings in a poem or painting.

❀ Reward yourself for trying so hard.

Everyone gets blue sometimes. Everyone faces disappointment—even Christians. But even when you don't get what you aim for, God's paying attention to the details of your life.

When you're sad or disappointed, there is something you can do about it. Share your disappointment with God through prayer. God wants you to talk to him about all your feelings—even the sad ones. He cares about how you feel. Besides that, getting your feelings off your chest is healthy.

After a disappointment, the time comes for you to try again.

The Bible shows God's promise to help us do just that.

Isaiah 40:29–31 says,

"He gives strength to those who are tired and more power to those who are weak. Even children become tired and need to rest, and young people trip and fall. But the people who trust the Lord will become strong again. They will rise up as an eagle in the sky; they will run and not need rest; they will walk and not become tired."

Imagine that! God knows that you will get tired and disappointed. He knows that sometimes you'll fail at something that's important to you. But the promise given here can help you try again. God is always ready to give you support and lend you strength to keep trying.

MESSAGE TO GOD

Dear Lord, it's really hard when things just don't go as I hoped. I look forward to your help. It's pretty awesome to know you're always there for me. Thank you, God. Amen.

Prayer Starters

Dear God, I just want to hide my head today because . . .

God, help me try again to . . .

Dear God, I'm still kind of sad. I will look to you for strength. I know that you are with me all through the day. Amen.

I was so disappointed about . . .

God helped me to start again by . . .

I believe God is always ready to help me because . . .

Sometimes I'm not certain about how I feel about God. Am I supposed to have some mushy feelings or something? I want to grow to love God more because I know that's what I'm supposed to do. How can I love God?

signed,

God's Valentine

MESSAGE TO GOD

Lord, I'm so thankful that I have your love and that I know you're with me. Please help me grow to love you even more. Amen.

tHinGS wE LoVe

- ⚘ Pizza
- ⚘ Best friends
- ⚘ Favorite music
- ⚘ Liver . . . no, just kidding!
- ⚘ Kittens

Matthew 22:37–39 says,

"'Love the Lord your God with all your heart, all your soul, and all your mind.' This is the first and most important command. And the second command is like the first: 'Love your neighbor as you love yourself.'"

Do you love pizza the same way that you love your mom? Of course not! Think about the ways we use the word love. You can see that love is used to mean a lot of different things. The kind of love we have for our friends is different from the way we love to eat pizza. The romantic love that husbands and wives have (or that "mushy" feeling boyfriends and girlfriends have) is another kind of love. But what kind of love does God show us? And how should we love God in return?

The Bible uses a Greek word to describe godly love. God's kind of love is called *agape.* Jesus is the best example of agape. He showed agape when he served others. He taught us that agape is making the feelings and wellbeing of others more important than our own feelings and wellbeing. The ultimate example of God's kind of love was when Jesus died to save us.

1 John 4:9 says,
"This is how God showed his love to us: He sent his one and only Son into the world so that we could have life through him."

When you love God, it's not some mushy feeling. It's an action! The way to love God is to love others. Let's look at some ideas about how you can "love your neighbor as you love yourself."

Ways to love God
1. Read to small children or the elderly.
2. Volunteer in the church nursery.
3. Lend a hand around the house.
4. Surprise someone with a little homemade gift.
5. Serve at a shelter or soup kitchen.

MESSAGE TO GOD

Dear God, your love is amazing. I know you are going to help me grow to love you and others. That is so cool! Thanks for giving me some great ways to share your love with people I know. Amen.

Prayer Starters

Lord, I feel so good today about . . .

God, I love you because . . .

God, please help me show your love to . . .

Today, God, I want to share your love. I'm going to try harder to see others as you see them. I am anxious to show how I love you. Thank you. Amen.

I'm showing God that I love him by . . .

God showed me this verse about love in his Word . . .

My family expresses love by . . .

Cool books for tweens!

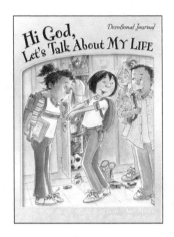

Hi God, Let's Talk About MY Life
Devotional Journal
written by Karen Ann Moore
0-7847-1246-8

Dear God, Let's Talk About YOU
Devotional Journal
written by Karen Ann Moore
0-7847-1247-6

Believe It!
Bible basics that won't break your brain
written by Steven James
0-7847-1393-6

Available now at your local bookstore!